Things of the Sea
Belong to the Sea

Things of the Sea Belong to the Sea

D. George

To Leigh Ann

Thank you for all of the wonderful book discussions! Happy Reading

J. A. Larrabee

BELLINGHAM
2010

iUniverse, Inc.
New York Lincoln Shanghai

Things of the Sea Belong to the Sea

Copyright © 2007 by D. George

All rights reserved. No part of this book may be used or reproduced by any means, graphic, electronic, or mechanical, including photocopying, recording, taping or by any information storage retrieval system without the written permission of the publisher except in the case of brief quotations embodied in critical articles and reviews.

iUniverse books may be ordered through booksellers or by contacting:

iUniverse
2021 Pine Lake Road, Suite 100
Lincoln, NE 68512
www.iuniverse.com
1-800-Authors (1-800-288-4677)

The views expressed in this work are solely those of the author and do not necessarily reflect the views of the publisher, and the publisher hereby disclaims any responsibility for them.

Cover photo: "A resident orca spyhops near Telegraph Cove, B.C." Photo by L.A. Larrabee

ISBN: 978-0-595-44227-0 (pbk)
ISBN: 978-0-595-88558-9 (ebk)

Printed in the United States of America

No one escapes the ravages of war behind closed doors.

Dedicated to all who have suffered from the ravages of war,
with the wish that in the Beauty and Wisdom of Art,
we may find Hope for Humanity.

ON FIELDS OF GREY REGRET

—based on an anonymous Civil War photo

On fields of grey regret, the bodies fall—
Good men all, and younger than the grass
That paints them green and black. How high must bone
Pile upon bone before the taste of brass

Legislates an end to the blood-letting?
The stones are red, the sky is red, the dawn.
A dead sun glints on rusty bayonets,
On bones the color of marble and broken slate.

On fields of grey regret, the bodies fall
In stony rows for no good reason at all—
And they are falling yet. How deep? How tall?

How long must the wind rustle a dead man's hair?
My fingers itch to scratch an ancient sore.
How smooth the faces of those who go to war!

TABLE OF CONTENTS

*If we compare the creation of ideas
in nuclear physics to the writing
of poetry, then we have to write
sonnets, not free verse*

—Murray Gell-Mann
Nobel Laureate in Physics
1991

A NOTE ON THE POETRY
AND HOW IT CAME ABOUT

PART I: Sonnets from Surfside

Once upon a time, there was a kingdom by the sea: a private beach with tall fences and guards that shouldn't have existed as it did, seeing that it was below the tide-line—according to US geodetic surveys. Someday, the experts predicted, Surfside would wash away.*

Sandwiched between two prosperous public-access beaches (Seal Beach and Sunset Beach), Surfside was a delightfully shabby, run-down place—what realtors called a "low-rent area" and the residents called a paradise. The spectacular surf (high-cresting waves, sometimes stacked-up ten deep) attracted surfers up and down the coast. Unable to approach by land (the guards, the fences, the private beach) they came in by droves from the sea, riding the long boards popular then, arriving among the schools of dolphin and seals, the flocks of pelicans and gulls that fed upon the deep and shallow off-shore reefs.

Surfside, then, was teeming with wild life: water birds and huge pink crabs, abalone and oysters; a rich variety of fish including the smaller blue and tiger sharks, considered a delicacy by surf-casters; the grunion runs, the schools of *bonitos* when the sea was red. At low-tide, the mudflats and tide pools were invaded by clam-bake devotees, with their blue enamel pots and black boots and spears. You could literally live off the sea, and some at Surfside did.

Surfside wasn't much to look at. It didn't have that "well-scrubbed," freshly-painted and landscaped-look its hardworking neighbors of other beaches were so proud of. Its three rows of houses (A, B, C) sheltered about a hundred during the winter, three-hundred during the tourist season. The winter residents (I lived there year-round for several years) were a bunch of assorted characters, independent and varied. They included artists and poets and engineers, carpenters and masons, road-workers, a song-writer, a writer of children's books, an Austrian psychiatrist, the director of the Los Angeles Port, two marine biologists and an anthropologist, plus a large number of retirees—senior-citizens, mostly—who still surfed and ocean-fished, docking their boats across the highway in what used to be a bay.

Surfside had (inside its gated, guarded main entrance) a small general-store of sorts with a jukebox and café tables. Across from it was a ten-car parking lot (often inundated with two feet of sand during high tide) which adjoined a tiny US Post Office.

Thanks to the kind-hearted generosity of its gentle post-mistress, I was able to receive forwarded-mail many years after I had left Surfside, letters sometimes forwarded with a note: "What are you doing in those weird places?"—referring to the odd addresses in London, Cairo, Istanbul, Marrakesh—and, finally, to my addresses in Spain, where I had settled down for twelve years.

In the tenth year, however, I was cut off by the advent of a new post-mistress who was not as gentle and kindhearted, who forwarded a final note: "That's it." And so I lost (in California) what I had come to realize was a simple and somewhat prestigious USA address: D. George, Surfside, California.

The government and its tide-survey experts were right of course. Things of the sea belong to the sea. Shortly after I left, Surfside lost a dozen or so of its houses fronting the sea on "A-row," including the one I had lived in, victims of a series of high-tides. The post office was spared and the general store, whose owner (a Yugoslavian political refugee) wrote me in German that not all was lost: "Bits and pieces of the lost houses are still sending us signals—a chair-leg here, a bed-post there."

"Not all is lost," he wrote. "All is well. Surfside is still standing. You won't recognize it, though. The engineers built a mole and the beach is silted up with sand a long way off. It looks like the Sahara. The ocean is a thin blue line on the horizon."

PART TWO: The Admiral of the Ocean Sea

During my years in Seville, Spain, I often dined in Triana, across the river from the *torre del oro*, the gleaming roof-tiled "tower of gold" beside the Guadalquivir where Columbus had docked, and where much of the gold from the Americas was unloaded and stored.

Even back then, I was thinking about Columbus. I had read his letters in the Archives, often stood before his enormous tomb in the Cathedral, often passed the statue of Rodrigo in a small plaza in Triana.

"Who's that?" I remembered asking a Gypsy when I first arrived. "Who is that young man shading his eyes with one hand and looking into the distance?"

"That's Rodrigo," the Gypsy replied. "He's the Gypsy from Triana who discovered America. He was the first to sight land."

Drawn by local legends and stories, I spent a week at the monastery, La Rábida, where Columbus had arrived from Portugal (with his son in hand) to seek advice from the Queen's confessor and to plot his journey. Nearby was Palos de la Frontera, now silted up, from which Columbus had sailed on his first voyage to America. His desk and cell are still in the monastery. The pulpit from which he spoke is still in the church at Palos.

A year later, I found myself at Sagres, the "Balcony of Europe" in Portugal, wandering the high cliffs above the Atlantic, wondering about Columbus. Here is where Prince Henry had his "School for Navigators." Here, in these ruins, is where Columbus had studied and stood, looking out upon the dark and unknown, forbidding, mysterious sea.

The next year, I went to Lisbon, where Columbus and his brother had a nautical books and maps establishment in the narrow, winding streets of the Old Section. Then I went to Salamanca, where Columbus had pleaded his case before the academicians there. And Cordobá, where he had lived, and had his audiences with the Queen. And Santa Fé, outside of Granada, where Columbus was when Granada fell, and where he was finally commissioned and funded to sail to America from Palos de la Frontera.

All the pieces were falling into place. During my year in Italy, I had stopped in Chios, where Columbus had taken on cargo in the early days of his sailing apprenticeship on the Mediterranean. Before that, I had looked around the Old Market in Istanbul (Constantinople) where he was reputed to have worked for the Genovese banking interests.

After awhile, it began to occur to me that I was doing a book on Columbus, a book that didn't begin to write itself until five years ago in Sacramento,

California. In Sacramento ("sacred place" in Spanish) I came across his *Book of Prophecy*, and the definitive, newly-translated books by Taviani.

Then I began to write—not about the school-book Columbus, but that other Columbus "on location," the shadowy figure that emerged far grander and compelling than I had anticipated. Five-hundred sonnets later, I went back to Spain to look around some more, to fill in some blank spaces.

The sonnets here in Part Two: The Admiral of the Ocean Sea, are excerpts drawn from my extensive narrative work, *Discovering Columbus* (not yet published). They refer to the sea, things of the sea that he had encountered, could not help but encounter and overcome.

We know he died in a monastery in Léon, still shouting orders from his deathbed—still searching, it is said, for a route to the Indies.

PART THREE: Ekphrastic Sonnets from the Sea

Ekphrastic poetry is, of course, the verbal representation of a visual art: painting, sculpture, and so forth. Painting and poetry have often been called "the sister arts." They go together, they complement each other. They can enhance each other, as they did during the Tang Dynasty, for example, when Chinese poet-painters often adorned their paintings with poems by themselves and others.

The sonnets here, drawn from my *Sonnets Pro Arte*, were selected because they refer to the sea. They include seascapes by Turner, Tahitian sketches by Gauguin, a nude bather by Renoir, a light-house by Edward Hopper. Dali is represented here by his *Contending Angels*, set on a Catalán beach; his strange version of the landing of Columbus; his odd but unforgettable *Portrait of Picasso*, painted at Pebble Beach; Matisse by his *Bathers with a Turtle* and *Moroccan Triptych*; Picasso by his *Lobster and Cat on the Beach*.

About thirty painters and forty ekphrastic sonnets and sonnet sequences appear in these pages, all drawn from *Sonnets Pro Arte*—a collection of ekphrastic poetry I have written over the years. *Sonnets Pro Arte* (unpublished) ranges in chronology from cave paintings, Chinese scrolls, Greek vases, Egyptian mosaics, to modern and post-modern contemporary painting. As stated before, only those poems and paintings which concern themselves with the sea, things of the sea, were culled from *Sonnets Pro Arte* to appear here.

This doesn't mean, of course, that the poetry and painting that appears in Part III are the *best* sea paintings by a particular painter, or the *best* ekphrastic sonnets I have written about the sea, based on the work of a particular painter. Space considerations and other factors came into play.

This is not primarily a book about sea-paintings or ekphrastic poems about the sea. The poems in the first part, *Sonnets from Surfside*, are mostly "free-standing" poems drawn directly from nature, from things of the sea that have affected me. Many of these are in the first person, in my own voice, as it were. I was there in the ebb and flow. I came upon the spider-crab, the sea-turtle, the shell leaning seaward in the sand. The dolphin in the sonnet "Dolphin" is a *real* dolphin that used to ride along with me, playfully nudging my surfboard between waves.

The poems in Part II: *The Admiral of the Ocean Sea*, are exclusively in the third person. I attempted to be faithful to the personality and character of Columbus (as I was able to understand them). The time I spent in waterfront bars and at sea among the sailors in Andalucían seaports and their counterparts in Portugal, Italy, Spain, and elsewhere, gave me some insights I couldn't have obtained as easily in San Francisco or New York.

The poems in the third section, "Ekphrastic Sonnets," presented a different set of problems. They were, in short: *being true to the painter's intention; being respectful of his subject-matter.* I believe that a truly ekphrastic poet should not "betray" the painter by manipulating or misrepresenting what he tried to do or did. I try not to deviate from what I understand to be the painter's intention. That is, I try not to use the painting as a "springboard" into *my* world, my *own* ego, my *own* intentions. I try to stay in *his* world, the painter's world, as a "mouthpiece" or interpreter if I can.

Those poets that pretend to be "ekphrastic": "I saw Brueghel's hunters and hounds/tromping the snow/among the trees/in Michigan/down by Grampa's cabin/it was Thanksgiving, I think …" can be found (too frequently) in would-be poetry magazines that do not care about what Brueghel cared about—or Leonardo, or Edward Hopper, for that matter. This also applies (by analogy or extension) to those "translators" who (as Robert Frost pointed out) *betray* the poetry of the original poet.

When I am "working" a painting (researching, gazing at, walking around in it), I try to "become" the painter: *What did he mean? What did he think and feel about this tall table, this chair? Why did he paint the apples purple?*

If I am very lucky, I will "meet" the painter on the stair. This happened with M.C. Escher, who walked me around one of his etchings, one of those mind-bending puzzles he was so fond of. It was more pleasant with Vermeer, who introduced me to his *camera obscura*, and explained how he achieved the luster of his pearly light—pure conjecture, of course.

In other words, the ekphrastic poet owes fidelity—as a point of honor—to the painter whose work he's working with. Also, the ekphrastic poet must enhance the painting with his verbal skill—or at least *try* to do so. To parody a painting by a dead painter is a petty undertaking at best. Either endorse it, do it honor, or let it rest in peace. Right or wrong, I always try to leave a painting better than when I found it—meaning, of course, by respecting its milieu, by working (in words) within the boundaries that the painter intended to be observed.

PART ONE

Sonnets from Surfside

Before Surfside, my childhood-poetry began on the shores of Lake Michigan at Milwaukee: the lake banks and beaches and woods of Bay View. Then came Germany: *Sonnets from Stuttgart* (since lost). Back in Milwaukee, *The Year of the Quiet Sun* and other books were written in the Pillsbury Manor coach house, high on the lake bank overlooking Milwaukee's North Shore Yacht Club. (The book of Chinese lyrics in English, *The Year of the Quiet Sun*, is now in the hands of a painter in Taiwan for Chinese-brush illustrations.)

Surfside, in my late twenties, was a revelation. I had never lived on the ocean before, certainly not on piers hanging over the water. High tide became a dramatic affair. Those were exciting years. *Sonnets from Surfside* was written there—some in Venice, on the Adriatic, some in Spain, in Cadiz, with its fifty-foot sea-wall on the Atlantic—but mostly on the Pacific at Surfside, California.

THINGS OF THE SEA BELONG TO THE SEA

The shell in my hand, no bigger than my fist,
Is closing down because it must exist.
Hinged like a drawbridge, its embattled gate
Guards the glow of its inner ornament—

The ghost of the oyster that activates the pearl—
The soul within, the world without the pale.
I run my fingers over its grooves and scars
Encrusted with lichen and barnacle and weed—

Medals won in combat, the outer war
It wages with the sea. I feel the tide
Surge around my ankles—on every side

Suction, pressure, a tugging intensity
Heightened by the grip of what I hold in my hand,
Surrender gently, and step back up on land.

THE BIRTH OF VENUS

When she was born, a wind was in the waves.
They crested high and white, as if the ocean
Felt the impact of something going on,
Something bright in the deep of its dark cave.

Trumpets blared. The mainsprings of their valves
Unleashed the yellow sound of another sun—
The one behind the eye, behind the shine
That radiated through her many lives.

What thing occurred, cried out, and then lay still
Upon the water in its womb of brine?
Pristine in spite of its passage through the green,

She must have been more than beauty, more than a pearl,
More than the freestanding figure of a woman
That Botticelli painted upon a shell.

BEAUTY

Sometimes unexpectedly, unbidden,
Beauty comes. Not a downpouring of doves,
Not a Venus, sheathed in an ivory shell,
Not even the lenses of Stonehenge in its season—

Stones aligned to catch the sun as it moves
Mystically, majestically, through holes
And crevices. Not even these spectaculars—
The light against the dark, the white ecstatic,

Stars falling and setting the sky on fire—
Take possession, or let the moment take
The horse high over the hedge with an unseen rider.

It comes when least expected, when the dark
Opens a crack to let light filter in—
A word, a look, a sudden realization.

By The Aquarium. Photo by L.A. Larrabee

AQUARIUMS

Aquariums begin with panes of glass
Tightly fitted to keep the water in.
Then come sand, and pebbles, and colored stone—
Snails and shells, and rocks with crevices

For the fish to hide in. And weeds, of course—
Vertical weeds that break the surface, and weeds
That merely float, and lights that emphasize
Bulging fish eyes, magnified by glass,

That push against and peer through barriers.
This is how aquariums begin.
This is how it all began—the sky,

The sea, the first breath of anything that is—
Beginning with the mind behind the eye
That loves like light what it illuminates.

FOUND-OBJECT

Tangled in seaweed, it glittered like a shell
That looked the worse for wear in that green thicket.
I picked it up and put it in my pocket
Because I wanted something impractical—

An afterthought, a little piece of bell
To jingle when I later took it out.
The knack of it eluded me. I thought
The simple act of possession would cast a spell,

Carry me out like driftwood in the tide
And cast me back alive with the thrill of it.
Not so. It had the look of porcelain—

Pocked and pitted—as if a dream had died,
As if the sea, in polishing that bone,
Had done the best with beauty that it could.

SEAWARD LEANS THE SHELL

Seaward leans the shell upon the land.
The tines of its fluted porcelain are bent
Toward the listing waves of its lament.
Gleaming with seawash, and salty in its span,

I hold this small dark chalice in my hand
As if the sea were riding in its spell,
As if this shell were more than empty shell
That I found tilting seaward in the sand.

Was it cast by accident or design
To look like a white hand reaching for the sea?
Perhaps there is more to mother-of-pearl than meets

The outer eye. Perhaps each particle,
Even dead barnacles on the backs of whales
Are part of the broken riddle of water and light.

THE DOLPHIN

To know the ocean as a dolphin does—
The easy motion of gliding through a wave
And out the other side, as if it has
Intuitive understanding of the laws

That govern surge and flow, the dolphin has
Refined itself. Nothing can slow its graceful
Slide through a running tide—its fins and tail
Send it surging into the wave's caress.

The dolphin is so intimate with surf
That each small wave, even the sea itself,
Glides within the green of a dolphin's brain.

It moves as the sea moves, rides each windy swell,
Leaps with the sea-bright skill of a dancer, until
The dance of dolphin and the wave are one.

IN THE BEGINNING IS THE UGLY

Not ugly because it is toadlike, only because
In the beginning of everything is the ugly:
The tadpole, the duckling, the frog before it is princely—
Dragons that grin with pink and pearly jaws.

The harsh incongruity of stark surprise
Flusters, shocks, delays receptivity.
The news is lost: the beauty behind the ugly,
Behind the look. The beauty I speak of defies

Analysis. It lies about things of the earth.
The bent bamboo, the drumbeat, the sucked-in breath
Come closer to definition than the word.

But who's to say what keyhole in the sky
Was cut to fit the eye that spies on God?
I listen to fish because they live in the sea.

THE SPIDER-CRAB

A spindly spider-crab with spokes for legs
Walks out upon the rocks I'm standing on.
Not far below, the tide is coming in—
A shapeless thing that surges, lingers, sags,

Climbs higher in a swirl of foam that marks
The sun-baked rocks with the dark of its design—
The same uncertain deck I'm standing on.
The spider-crab seems unconcerned with the sea,

Steps stiffly out upon a shifting rock—
A hunter stalking what a hunter seeks.
The sea explodes with spray where the spider stood,

And washes down a web of shell and weed.
The rocks are wet and gleaming in the sun
But suddenly empty, now that the spider's gone.

Drawing by D. George

THE UNICORN

When first I came upon the unicorn—
The sea behind it calm as wind-blown glass—
I scoffed at the pretense of its gilded horn.
But then it stamped and neighed, and I was afraid

That even apparitions—splendid beasts—
Are bred by the gods for devious purposes.
Call the hunters, call the quivering hounds.
Yellow coronets call down the sun

To witness where a unicorn has run.
When I looked back upon where it had been,
I saw the tracks of a white and glistening horse

That leaped into the tide. The sky was black.
A lazy gull was swallowed by a cloud
That swelled to immense proportion until it died.

THE SEA-TURTLE

The turtle shell lay gaping in the sand.
Inverted like a bowl, or a small boat,
And peeled by the sea down to its outer coat,
It once enclosed a turtle-soul that spawned

A turtle-body that swam and waddled on land.
But now the turtle, ragged and remote,
Lies naked on a crest of sand apart.
Far from the weedy crash of tide, it lies stranded

High on the beach where the sea abandoned it.
I came upon this echo of a turtle
While walking a beach where gulls were loud in the sun.

Schools of dolphin were leaping in white swells,
And all was alive and well, except for one—
Nothing but shadow in an empty shell.

BLUE MUSSELS

> The mussels hung dull blue and
> Conspicuous, yet it seemed
> A sly world's hinges had swung
> Shut against me.
> > —Sylvia Plath, from
> > "Mussel Hunter at Rock Harbour"

The mussel gripped the pier and held its breath—
Fuzz on its lips and slime on its shell, the tide
Sucking as if it were starved to death for mussels.
Clumping together like brides at a clam-bake, they cling

Tight to their perch high out of the water—
The waves reaching, coming back empty-handed,
The mussels gleaming ebony in the wave-wash,
Smacking their lips in the sweet brine of their birth.

What is it with blue mussels? They hide their orange—
The tight-fisted muscle that clings to mother of pearl—
Strangely seated, as if orangutans

Ate their fill of mussels and walked away—
The tide complaining, the mussels sucking air,
Taking advantage of a single appendage.

SIGHTING REALITY THROUGH THE NECK OF A BOTTLE

When tilted toward light, another kind of world
Reflects the work of salt and a grinding sea.
The glass is etched. A bright reality
Burns in the turning at the tunnel's end.

Is this the shard of a wayward star in my hand?
It flares in its flaws, like the sun in the glass of Chartres.
Perhaps a message from an uncharted planet
Was bottled in space and cast into solar wind

To land where it has fallen in the sand.
Or is it only what it seems to be?
For here are the marks of the pouring, the marks of the mold,

Benchmarks of the glazier's art that seize
The smallest error, magnify each flaw,
Making a maze through which the mind can flow.

STAINED-GLASS IN A CRYSTAL PARADISE

Like smoke and cloud, opaque but delicate,
They interchanged in thought and attitude
Untouched transparencies. Alike in mood,
They understood the misting of the light

That left their flesh in shadows at their feet.
There was no night, no death; ingratitude
Had not been invented yet. What did they do
To occupy the intervals between

Fruit and flower, the wave's caress, the flow
Reflected in the even glow of sun
Upon their skin? It strains the imagination

To think of them alone in infinite space—
Lightly attired, and stepping gently around
The green-eyed gardener dozing in the grass.

THE ISLAND DRAWN FROM MEMORY

She drew an island, then she drew a boat—
The sea surrounding both, the water green.
Then she drew a tree. She made it lean
Inward, islandward; it seemed to float

In its own sphere, as if it had a root
Independent of the island scene.
She was the tree: a stately palm, serene,
With elegant, tapering leaves. She was the boat

Floating off the shore. She was the sea, the waves,
The gentle motion of water against the hull.
She was the island, too, in other lives,

And sensed the meaning of each particle—
The sand above and pearl below the sea.
She drew and drew until she was all of these.

REFLECTIONS ON A SHAPELY FORM IN FLIGHT

In order for there to be a mirror of the world
it is necessary that the world have a form.
— Umberto Ecco, *The Name of the Rose*

What if the world were formless—what would there be
To shine upon itself, shape meaning, sight?
What is light without shadows to reflect—
Look back upon, regret? Nothing but sky—

An abstract emptiness. Reality
Needs a fact to demonstrate a fact:
The bee, the flower, the moving silhouette.
A hawk alighting in a barren tree

Mirrors—in light rays—what a hawk can be.
Thinking of these things, I cast a stone
Skipping over the surface of a pond.

The stone transformed in flight—the stone became
A silver disk that skittered before it fell
Into a dim reflection of itself.

THE SHAPE OF THINGS

The ever-expanding curve of things to come
Began to move before the earth was born.
It arches over everything. Each line
Bends to fit the arc of what it is,

And stretches into what it will become.
The shapes of things determine what they are:
Perfect spheres of falling water fall
In shapes that never vary from the norm.

A circle is born when air and water form
Mute alliance within a molecule.
Soul is circle. How could it be square?

Towers lean, but circles float in air.
And tons of snowflakes, falling on a pond,
Become, in fact, what they are falling on.

DEATH SQUARED

If death is squared with the shape and speed of light,
Can it be equated with other things in space?
If years are measured by incandescent flight,
What hour is this? Perhaps some other place

Looks like this, like earth, but is out of focus—
Impinging with pale prints, subliminal traces—
Like mountains that fall upon the valley floor
And flower there, and flower in the sea,

As if the fact of falling doesn't matter
To immortality. The twisted tree—
Gnarled in its rock, and garlanded in air—

Does it give thought to the kind of fruit it bears?
And where is death, when sour apples fall
From dizzy heights to sweeter ports of call?

GALAXIES

I think of galaxies now in the brain's marrow—
Minute apostrophes that register pain,
Sorrow, and other things that move within the bone.
I think of planets within the cells that flow—

The shapes of their changing character, and how—
In the last analysis—their needs are plain:
Dolphins in a running tide, or field sparrows,
Or dark-eyed children standing in the snow.

I think of that vast, invisible terrain
Peopled by the brain's imagination
That moves in me, and flows in the same skull

I co-inhabit with the intangible.
I think of black umbrellas in the rain,
And butterflies that flutter in the sun.

Drawing by D. George

PINS AND WHEELS: A METAPHYSICAL

Do stones in the crystal chambers of their souls
Move without meaning in their molecules?
Do even the smallest, the insignificant least—
Like dust on the tusk of the most revolting beast—

Detect in the flesh of the invisible
A sense of purpose? If souls have knees that kneel,
And stones have brains that calculate the cost
Of energy, then even the busy flea—

Vastly underrated by the cat—
Plays a part in a delicate balancing act:
The pins and wheels that keep the world afloat.

Now when I feel the pitch and tilt of an ark
That I have been riding too lightly in the dark,
I praise the water flowing under my feet.

STONE

Somewhere among us a stone is taking notes.
   —Charles Simic, *Heaven Bone*, 1989

Stone has so deep a sense of its certainty,
It seems to sleep when others lie awake
Staring like owls, because they cannot speak
Of what they cannot see. Stone doesn't try

To scale a height, or sail a glassy sea
To touch eternity's face behind the mask
Ulysses wore, or Icarus, nor does it ask
Why it is lying so quietly in its shell,

Nor does it seem aware of other souls
Stirring in space beyond its molecules.
Stone stands still in the pool of its solitude—

In striking contrast to that immortal clay
Shifting indecisively, with mind and eye
Only half open, and still unsynchronized.

WHALE-WATCHING FROM AN OPEN BOAT

Their rising always comes as a surprise.

The sea is calm, and then a whale appears—
Breaks surface, waves awash in its wake.
The mist of its blowhole drifts away, as it sucks
Fresh air in.
             In spite of the surf, I can hear
The suffing sound of its breathing as it blows.
I'm close enough to see how drops of water
Cling like pearls in the ridges of its eyes.

I study whales. Perhaps they study me.
I sense they need the vast immensities
Of open sea, unbroken distances

To think about, to sing their mournful songs in—
Even as I, by watching them, transcend
The cluttered canyons my intelligence moves in.

JACK-SALMON

I caught a salmon whose wings were severed, and fins
Jutted out of its backbone. I saw it leap—
The hook implanted deeply in its jaw—
And netted it half in water, half in dream,

Its body arched and curving away from me.
"That's a big Jack, buddy. It's still fighting the hook."
The guy on the left was leaning over to look.
"Torn up some, but there's still plenty to smoke."

And then I was a salmon, back in the bay,
Fresh from the sea and running upstream to spawn,
Feeling the fight and color go out of me.

As dawn turned to day, and the day was drained of its light,
I was still leaping barriers—rock over rock—
Leaping, leaping, leaping in spite of the hook.

LOW TIDE IN PORTUGAL

Neptune of the blood, O his frightening trident,
The dark wind in the breast of the coiled shell.
　　　　—Rilke, *The Third Elegy*

Nobody guards them: the women, the fleshy girls.
High on the wave's edge, in flowing skirts and veils
They go in two's and three's among the rocks—
Tridents ready to pitch into shore-birds and fish.

The old ones in shawls with cracked, enamel pails,
Poke around in the tide-pools, and under rocks
For squid and shell-fish, spider-crabs and shark—
Impaling them, squirming, in a single stroke.

At first, I didn't see the man hunched in the grass—
Closer than I to their tangle of baskets—
But one old lady did. Lifting her trident

She shook it at him and shouted obscenities—
Turning the others, who took up a trilling chant
Until he slid back into the sand-dunes, and vanished.

A TIME FOR SOARING AND FOR FALLING BACK

I saw a star that fell into the dark:
A blaze of light, and then it was no more—
As if in the soaring it had lost its spark,
Fell back upon the undemanding air.

So it is with soaring, the falling back
Upon a place where dark and endless space
Cools the ardor—a falling star that takes
Time to fall beyond the fire-place.

The floor of the valley is littered with meteors
That blazed for an instant and fell into the deep
Of what they were. So it is with the warrior

That burns with a holy fire, the child in sleep,
The lady in black, the bride on the widow's walk,
The man in grey who meets himself coming back.

GALAPAGOS OPTIONAL

Cruise the world on a clipper ship.
Long and short sea-journeys to exotic places.
Galapagos optional.
          —from an ad in the *New Yorker*

On this sea-journey, there was nothing but joy.
The first night out, they noticed that the stars
Lit up the sky with their own bright industry,
Some of them leaving markers in the air

Where dark had been before. The silver night—
Straight out of Velásquez—assembled there
Schooners and galleons, a billowing fleet of clouds
That disappeared as quickly as it came.

Did you see that? the lover came up for air.
See what? She mumbled, and pulled him down by the hair.
All night long, the dolphins followed the ship—

Leaping for pleasure, leaping just to leap;
While up on deck, in a corner of the bow,
Coils of rope were lying about like lovers.

THE SEA IS WAITING, LIKE PENELOPE

The sea is turning over under its breath
The broken bones of shells and sea-struck men
Who went to sleep with the taste of sand in their mouth.
The sea leans back and weaves a tapestry

Of green and weedy tide, a tattered shroud
Of intricate brocade. The ships of Troy
Still adrift in the myth of a stony sea,
Shift in their sandy caskets, under a grey

Revolving canopy, a cryptic sky
That speaks in signs that sailors recognize.
The sea says nothing. It rolls in the wind and weeps.

The wife on the widow's walk understands the sea.
She knows the mist, the sting of salt on her face.
The weariness of being old and deep.

BEYOND THE BEACH

Beyond the beach, where waves are laced with weed,
The broken walls of sunken cities stand
In blue exile. What did they call this land
That sank beneath a sudden rush of tide?

Fish are feeding where a temple stood.
On marble altars, deep in shell and sand,
Dolphins are carved in black obsidian.
Where are the street-signs, where are those who died

Reaching for each other in the tide?
Now divers sift through skull and scattered bone
Searching in silence for gold and silver coin.

They do not care whose bones are in the mud,
Whose blood is in the briny of the sea—
Nor do the fish, feeding on green jade.

LOOKING FOR ETRUSCANS

You see them everywhere, calmly invisible.
In seaports and the wooded hills of Rome,
Their sculpted heads and enigmatic smiles
Decorate small cafés, adorn the tombs

Of aristocracy. Their frescos are
Drenched with color, delirious with joy.
Dolphins and dancers are leaping in the air
As if a trick of choreography

Had taught them how to dangle there forever.
Some say the gods—engraved upon their clay—
Were far too beautiful to disappear

Without a trace of what they were doing here;
As when—in a rapture of splendor and surprise—
Their dying became as stunning as their lives.

THE LASSITUDE OF ULYSSES

How dull it is to pause, to make an end,
To rust unburnished, not to shine in use!
  —Tennyson, "Ulysses"

The lassitude of Ulysses—fair hand at making
The sea caress him, the crew come to his call,
Lashed out at his wife's suitors: he slew them all.
And what did Homer have him do then? Not a thing.

It ends in a wine-cup: the flesh of a stuffed-ox and song—
Barbaric howling, the walls of a great hall hung
Red and dripping, the heads of a kingdom impaled,
The wine-god jesting with his harsh underling:

Cup by cup contesting, keeping his courage up
Against the day the sea drained out of his sails.
Penelope knew. She tucked in the threads of her grief,

Spindled in homespun a sheath for the terrible knife
Slicing, slicing, the man and the wife in half—
Until he fit the garment that she had woven.

PART TWO

Admiral of the Ocean Sea

The sea-sonnets that follow have been drawn from a long narrative work, *Discovering Columbus*. Only sonnets relating to the sea are included here. Drawn from different sections of a tightly-constructed chronological narrative of 500 sonnets and sonnet-sequences, they are lifted out of context by necessity.

The first sonnet, for example, is not the first sonnet in *Discovering Columbus*. The first sonnet that appears here is drawn from a chapter on his first voyage.

THE OCEAN SEA

Looking for centers at the edges of thought,
He often stood at the wind's periphery
Feeling the sails fill up, the mast quiver.
When nothing's there to focus on, the sea

Unfolds its own deceptive blue and grey—
Its indigos of shadows, underneath
What ships pass over, the shape of it, the sand
Thrown upward by the wind into the stars—

The same sand blowing back again to fall
Like jewels upon the velvet of the deep.
There's always hope, there's always a time to sail

Around the tip of another planet's tail.
It's coming back that matters—the cool and dark,
When all the world is burning up with light.

THINKING ABOUT HIS CASE IN SALAMANCA

It wasn't as if he had stepped out into the dark
Hoping to put his foot down on a ledge—
The waters closing behind him, as if a door
Opened and closed on command, as it did for Moses,

Landfall looming up with mountains and peaks
Bright and apocalyptic, the curving shore
Steaming with shellfish baked in a fire-pit.
It seemed self-evident—given the distance run—

That land would be standing where he landed, where
It lay as a certainty—yellow against the grey
Of Martîn's globe, of Toscanelli's map.

All he had to do was guide his ship
Into the harbor—if he could find a harbor
Nestled among the islands on the map.

THE WATERSPOUT

—from his journal of Voyage IV (1502–1564)

They stood at the rail together, two tall men,
Leaning on elbows folded precisely as wings.
Each was aware of something in the air—
Worlds in collision, a comet, a shooting star.

They stood at the rail, father and son, as if
It took four eyes to see what they wanted to see.
The ocean hissed in its harness. Overhead,
Clouds of all ages were corrugating the sky.

And then what happened? Fernando brought him back.
They killed each other—the Spanish, the Indians.
That's what I heard, Fernando said. *I was shocked.*

They stood in silence, and then Fernando said
I heard about it first in court. The King
Said it was just another brave new world.

II

Columbus laughed. *The King knows nothing about*
Ruling a country that doesn't even exist.
No world is brave that has such people in it,
Or new because it abides in its own design.

Again they were silent. A sudden wind came up.
The ship creaked. The rigging began to whine.
The King, Fernando said, *depends upon*
Too many men of dubious reputation.

The King's men, Columbus said, *degrade*
The ground they stand on. Do you remember when
One of them threw me in chains? Fernando frowned.

And Uncle Bart. I was but ten at the time.
Old enough, Columbus said, *to decide*
None of them are worth trusting with your life.

III

A waterspout was twisting out of the south.
Jesus, Mary, and Joseph—what is that?
That, my son, is a waterspout, he said.
The crew was up and about, crowding the rail.

The lookout was shouting. Rain began to fall
Lightly at first, then in a sudden burst
Drenching Columbus and every man on deck.
Go below, Columbus said to Fernando.

Fernando looked stricken. *I can't see it below.*
Then go to my cabin and get my Bible, he said.
The Bible did it, the captain's bellow, or both.

The spinning tower of water veered off and died—
Collapsed in its tower, as if the verses had
Driven the apparition to its knees.

THE HURRICANE HE PROPHESIED

—from the journal of August 30, 1502

They should have listened. They might have lived to tell
How the hurricane passed them by that night.
Columbus alerted Ovando to the fact
A cyclone was coming. He felt it in his bones.

Then he took shelter at Puerto up the coast.
Columbus was not mistaken. Ovando was.
The oily waves, the inconsistent tide,
The sudden, swelling sea—all overcame

Ovando's fleet, which was tossed about like twigs
Splintered on rocks, or thrown upon the beach.
No one survived. Not one of the twenty ships.

The Lord had punished his bitterest enemies:
Bobadilla, the man who had clamped him in chains;
Francisco Roldán, the courtier who had betrayed him.

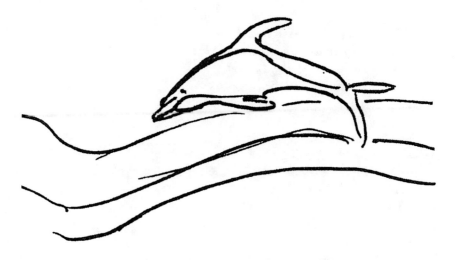

Drawing by D. George

BECALMED FOR THREE DAYS

We have begun to see large patches of
yellowish-green weed, which seems to have
been torn from some island or reef.
                    —arriving in the Sargasso Sea,
                The log for 17 September, 1492

They wondered at the teeming numbers of crabs
Undisturbed by foreign competitors—
But then a shadow fell across their nest.
They fled at his coming (he caught a few)

And hid among the blades of weedy debris—
Truly pelagic, that floated without root—
The Wandering Jew of the sea. He noted that
One end grew green. What wilted at the other,

Flourished and fed the fish, the water birds
Dipping their beaks in the rich and weedy brine.
But it, too, passed. They sailed through all of it,

Nothing impeding their passage. They were free
To follow terns and petrels, the frigate birds—
Birds of the sea that also rode the wind.

II

Birds of the sea that also rode the wind
Followed him, as he was following them.
They do that, sir, the pilot said, as he turned
To ask the pilot about the phenomenon—

Anything, to take his mind off the weed
Clogging the prow, the lookout said, the crew
Crowding the rail to see the grassy lake—
The green and yellow meadow, matted and thick,

That clung to the rudder, rustled beneath the hull.
I don't see a break, sir, the pilot said.
Stay on course, Columbus ordered. *Hang more sail—*

Hearing again the words of de Velasco:
Forge on, he said, *no matter how you feel.
Soon the sea will part, as it did for Moses.*

III

The flagship was too slow. It rode the wave
Steady but low in the water. Barnacles
Seemed to blossom in seas becalming and warm—
Dusky waters, dark as a gathering storm.

The Captain began to notice some of the men
Muttering low among themselves, about
Stone torsos rising, eyes with pupils of stone,
White hands reaching for moonlight in the weeds.

It's just superstition, the gunner's mate said.
He believed in nothing, not even dreams—
The hidden things of another sea beneath

This green thicket. *It's nothing,* he proclaimed.
Dolphins, maybe. To illustrate, he aimed
His crossbow at the flash of a passing fin.

43

IV

His mind was not becalmed. There were the waves
Lapping gently, the weed-entangled waves
Lapping incessantly at a wall of wood
Tilting into a tenement of sails. The sky—

Uninspired by anything but the sun,
Leaned over lightly to let its weight hang down.
There was, in the end, nothing to do but wait—
And this he did, pacing his cabin, his tread

Heavy upon the men in the bunks below,
Dozing between watches. Nobody said
Waiting was easy, nor did they say the road

Billowed out smartly all the way to Cathay.
Nor did anyone doubt the Captain was
Quick to exploit the slightest sliver of wind.

V

What did he discover, as he crossed over
The teeming bridge of sea-brocaded jade?
The common weed of innocence, whose chord
Clings to the stubborn ship, the voyager,

Leaves its tangled tentacles matted forever
Upon the Captain's bloated belly of pride.
It slowed him down. It cheated him of Speed.
So did the purple squid, the octopus,

The beauty of permanent ink staining the glass—
The last measure of stone, the untread tile
Cast on the shore of a shell-impacted tide.

Who walks now in the shallows, leaving no wake—
No indentation, not even the smallest print
To indicate the passage of horse and rider?

HE NAVIGATED BY DEAD RECKONING

He navigated by dead reckoning—
By watching bubbles of foam, by sniffing the air,
By sensing the sea's moods, the flights of birds,
By watching the time it took a stick to float

From bow to stern. He also watched the sky—
Navigated like Ulysses, observing
The transmutations of land and sea, the stars
Homer and Virgil accounted for, within

The blue *piazza*, the watery fishbowl called
The Mediterranean. But it took more
Than ancient lore to sail into solitude,

To conquer distance and loneliness and death,
To line up a shoreline with nothing but what he had
Aligned in his mind's eye, cradled in his head.

THE SEA WAS LIKE A RIVER, THE AIR SWEET

—a little over two-thirds of the way, Voyage I

> *The sea was like a river,*
> *the air sweet and very soft.*
> —the ship's log of September 26, 1492

The sea was smooth and calm. The caravels
Slid along with their sweeps, the oarsmen bent
Lightly to their task: there was no wind
Whistling in the rigging, no rushing sea

To pull against. Day after day, they had
Wind on the stern, but little of it to fill
The flapping mainsail, strapped against the mast.
Some went swimming. Some of them fished for food,

Delighted to hook a dolphin or a shark
To grill on the cooking box. But there was not
Enough to keep the grumblers occupied.

They lounged about in surly clusters, and glared
Whenever the Captain turned around, as if
To measure him for a wet and sudden end.

II

After three-thousand nautical miles, they found
Hand-carved canes, and a branch with a little flower
Not unlike the dog-roses in Castile
That bloom on hedges there. The men forgot

All their grievances, in the excitement of
Being the first to sight a tip of land
Leaping into view, a mountain peak
Silhouetted against the disk of sun

Sliding into the sea. By sunset, they
Had said their prayers and sung the *Salve Regina.*
Columbus, from the stern castle, made a speech

Reminding them they were hired by the Queen
To plant the banners of the expedition
With dignity, for God and Country and Crown.

RECONNOITERING CUBA

—from the journal of the first voyage, October 24, 1492

Navigating by day with line in hand,
They anchored within sight of land at night—
Alert to the splashing of paddles, the sudden thunk
Of wood on wood, the clunk of a thrown rope.

Nobody dozed on duty after that
First encounter with a painted face
Peeking over the rail's edge, or a lance
Stuck in the planking, a jagged arrow-head

Clattering in a corner of the deck.
And nobody slept, after that, without expecting
A shower of arrows arching out of the dark

Intent on finding targets, but no less
Than Dias endured, or Da Gama, with his fleet
Plundering villages off the African coast.

II

The fishhooks, the barkless dogs, the bone harpoons
Disappointed the gold hunters, the gods
Disembarking from the bowels of a bird
With drooping canvas wings. They stepped ashore

As if the beach were theirs, the native huts
Storehouse of buried booty, of charts
Marking each cache in blood, as pirates did.
Columbus strode at the head of an armed force.

Ready with sword and halberd. How could he know
The natives had nothing but sharpened sticks and spears
That pierced the smallest fish, the slowest iguanas?

Most of the Cuban coast was tangled with brush.
In many places, the mangrove was so thick
Not even a Spanish cat could slip through it.

THE SOUND OF LATIN

All was divided: the night, the day, the sea
Clinging to driftwood, the driftwood clinging to it.
Like bits of weed, the three ships seemed to drift
Across the face of what was—biblically—

A blue estate, a blue eternity.
At first light, the rigging still wet with mist,
The men were on their feet and breaking their fast—
Hardtack, blessed by the Captain who led them in song:

Salve, Regina, Mother of Mercy,
Our life, our sweetness, and our hope.
Save us from the terrors of the sea!

Were they ever aware of the irony—
The sound of Latin, the drone of Gregorian chant
Drifting across the changing face of the deep?

PILOTAGE

Tide was a major factor in pilotage
On the Atlantic. But who could measure time?
It could be reckoned only roughly at sea.
The crude, illiterate sailors memorized

Not the time, but the age and compass-bearing
Of the moon at high tide—that streak of light
Shining on the surface of the sea—
An obvious and dramatic track, whose bearing

Even they could observe and calculate
Without Latin, or charts, or geometry;
Which, of course, led to mutiny or worse—

The grinding of teeth behind the Admiral's back,
The arguments about pilotage, and rank
Pinzón settled with one hand on his sword.

LAND WAS A LIGHT
THAT FLICKERED AND FELL

—from the journal of the first voyage

Midway in flight, the current caught their keel
Cutting a swath through green and yellow weed—
Moving slow, at walking speed, their wings
Hanging limp in the middle of a sea

Riddled with algae, with brown bladders, with grapes
Floating on top of watery vineyards
As far as the eye could see, while overhead
Petrels descended, flitted above the waves,

And flying fish came flopping over the bow.
That was before the *Pinta's* captain saw
A towering cumulus cloud, and called it land.

Six nights later, the Admiral saw a light
"Like a wax candle," that flickered and rose and fell.
But after a while there was nothing, nothing at all.

II

At 2 AM, the full moon black with birds,
A sailor cried out from the *Pinta* that he saw
Land ahoy—a mountain dead-ahead—
A real mountain, not the shadowy

Unsubstantial castle-in-the-air
Wishes and greed conspire to invent;
Not the Indies, not the Flickering Light
Prophets and mystics carve into monuments;

Just a spark behind a garden wall
Branching out in new directions, its will
Independent of what expired before

Light flared, an ocean parted, a man
Walked on water, walked on the face of the moon,
Leaving footprints not even the wind erases.

Drawing by D. George

PART THREE

Ekphrastic Sonnets from the Sea

Drawn from *Sonnets Pro Arte*, an ever-expanding work I have been writing for years, the sonnets included here refer to the sea in its many manifestations. They, in turn, are based on paintings about the sea (and things of the sea) by 30 different painters, some of whom have devoted themselves to the sea (Turner, for instance, who has thousands of watercolors and oils in public and private collections) and others—Dégas, Guston, Vermeer, Chagall—who didn't use the sea as their central motif, citing the sea—for the most part—*en passant*.

Vermeer's *Geographer*, the first painting dealt with, begins this section of *Things of the Sea*, not only because it follows the section on Columbus, but also because of its centrality as a painting concerned with exploration, a singular and unique example (as is *The Astronomer*) of his preoccupation with scientific matters within the framework of his limited *oeuvre*. Dali, in contrast, often employed the sea as a motif. His *Persistence of Memory* was set on a Catalán beach. My long poem on this painting had to be left out of this section for reasons of space.

Rousseau is included tangentially, as are Rembrandt and Monet (who often painted the sea). Goya's famous dog is included in a Turner seascape. Matisse's *Bathers with a Turtle* (also referred to as *Three Women by the Sea*) is followed by Renoir's nude: *Blonde Bather*. Manet's studies of harbors are followed by his astonishing *On the Beach*. Then come Picasso's *Lobster and Cat*, Boudin's lady in white, Guston's *Green Sea* (1976) and Gauguin's *Tahitian Sketches*. The Joseph Stella included here utilizes Hart Crane's lines about the Brooklyn Bridge for added resonance. Hopper is represented here with three American paintings about the sea, Munch with two, Van Gogh with one, Chagall with two, M.C. Escher with two. This section finishes with a sonnet-sequence based on Courbet and Monet, ending with a single sonnet, *Monet's Last Request*, based on his seascapes from Normandy and a poignant letter to Renoir.

55

Drawing by D. George

THE GEOGRAPHER

—an oil on canvas by Vermeer, 1668

> ... *the air turns giddy with possibility,*
> *as though a whole new territory in the*
> *mind had been suddenly opened.*
>> —Louise Glück, explaining how
>> art serves the spirit in her 1993
>> essay "Voices."

Standing heavily at a table, he leans
Upon a rolled-up yellow chart, his arm
Bent at the elbow, his forearm resting, as he
Leans forward with dividers in his hand.

A wooden box supports his other hand—
A book, a block, a marker for the chart—
As he looks up and out into the street.
Things in the room about him are undisturbed:

The nautical map, the chest, the ornate chair
Calmly stand where they are. A timelessness
Pervades the room, the quiet atmosphere

Shattered by a shouting in the street.
What could that be? What's going on out there?
Concentration shattered, he looks up.

II

He pauses in his calibrations, and looks
Out of his window into the outer world.
Something strange is occurring in the street.
Above his head, the globe is undisturbed.

The charts upon the wall are still in place.
Is there anything out there? Do his eyes
Track the little as well as the grandiose?
A continent of ice is shifting gears

Far to the north. It makes a needle swing.
Far to the south, too far for human ears,
Tectonic plates are grinding underneath

A land of tundra, with foxes and migrating birds.
His maps show nothing. His charts are barren and void,
As if the earth were empty on each end.

III

Emptiness were no sin—*unless*, he thinks,
The "ends of the earth" were merely an empty phrase
Exploration could change. *Where are the men
That used to ride the wave wherever it led?*

That's what Columbus thought, when he started out
Thinking his way on paper. Graphs and charts
Could only go so far. He wanted to prove
Land was closer than anybody thought.

All it would take is a couple of boats to show
The barrier is mostly mental—the land
Lies there waiting quietly in the trees

That line the shore, the waves lapping at sand.
For a long time, the Dutch geographer
Stands at the window, pensively looking out.

IV

For a long time he stood there, looking out
Upon a world that wasn't invented yet.
What could he lay his quaint dividers against
That had not yet been tainted by a thought,

Painted over by blind painters, and bent
Into shapes no longer relevant?
For a long time he stood there, thinking about
Pristine beaches, and trees along the shore—

Things that change as the eye changes. He saw
Fleas on a cat's tail, islands of weed, a peak
Jutting out of an ocean that appeared

Gleaming and green, as if it were waiting for
The brooding stare of a sailor, looking out
Upon a beach that had never seen a boot.

V

Stars are stars, he thought. They set their clocks
By what the night is doing to the light
Allotted to the space surrounding them.
Sticks are sticks, and stones are stones, but what

Divides them into country, planet, globe
Is still unknown. He thought about the world
Divided into purely fictional parts.
He had the tools, of course, to plot a route

From where he's standing into anywhere—
But men to follow it? He closed his book.
It was too dark to see. Approaching dusk

Began to draw a curtain on the day.
Doubt was heavy in his heart, as he
Began to plot a voyage to the stars.

MOSES PARTING THE RED SEA

—an oil on canvas by Rembrandt (1606–69)

> *And Moses stretched out his hand over the sea;*
> *and the Lord caused the sea to go back by a*
> *strong east wind all that night, and made the*
> *sea dry land, and the waters were divided.*
> —Exodus

When he rode up, he could sense its immensity.
Unlike the mountain, which reared up under him,
The sea just lay there snarling, as the storm
Pelted it with hailstones, random pieces of sky.

Behind him, the sound of trumpet and drums
Terrified people, the huddled masses, who
Began to panic, milling around at his feet.
He never meant to subdue the quivering wave,

Only contain its raging long enough
To let his people pass. And this he did,
Raising it up and letting it fall away,

His people passing between its glittering teeth.
And Moses said: *Come here. Lie down. Be good!*
Stroking that which he could stroke of the sea.

THE DISCOVERY OF AMERICA BY CHRISTOPHER COLOMB

—an oil on canvas, by Dali
(1958/1959), now in Cleveland

When Dali painted the landing of Colomb,
Did he believe in the innocence of the quest?
Behold the man as a christ in his winding sheet,
A boy in swaddling clothes. His right hand grips

The mast of Mary's banner, the *sin pecado*,
As if he were planting it on the edge of what
The new world was, what he wanted it to be:
A holy enterprise. His left hand grips

The magic wand of leadership, the stick
Moses tapped a rock with to make it gush
Baptismal water, water out of a stone.

Clearly Dali was dealing with miracles—
With skeletal portents in a distant sky;
With prophecy, with the aspirations of Rome.

II

Let it not be forgotten that a cross
Impelled all this: Christ as an albatross,
His arms extended like wings, his blood-stained face
Wetly etched as it was on the Turin shroud.

Across from it, a Murillo effigy
Stands in her toga and halo, her folded hands
Clamped together devoutly. Did he paint
Mary like this (a goddess of mercy) because

He had taken a vow of penitence, when
The seas were not as calm as they are now?
Behind her are lances—the pikes and lances and flags

Velasquez painted at the surrender of Breda.
Behind her are banners and more banners, as if
The sea is much more turbulent than we think.

III

When Dali painted the landing, he didn't ignore
A bishop with his miter blessing the ship.
Nor did he ignore the naked sailors
Clutching banners—a purification rite—:

John the Baptist with olive branches and doves.
All the water that day was virgin and holy.
The ship standing at anchor with bleeding sails,
Proudly displays her blind oblivion—

Each rent and tatter patched and ready, as if
She were just standing idle, waiting for wind.
Is that the monkish soul of Columbus, crouched

Beneath the ship, an ornate cross in his hand?
He cowers behind the golden body of Christ—
Priming the pump, as it were, with Spanish gold.

IV

Humble Columbus. The landing of Colomb.
Naked men become again as boys
Bearing banners and crosses. Did they fear
An overload of the senses when they landed

Upon a beach as beautiful as this?
Look at all the silver they're leaving behind!
The sea is silver, the figures in the clouds
Thread the sky with silver. Their shadows fall

A great distance—as when Columbus leaps
Into his shadow, grotesque on the golden shore.
About to step on his shadow, does he note

The barnacle-studded capsule at his feet?
Or is he too involved in leaping, to see
The empty shell of an older enterprise?

V

The sky's the thing, the sea. It always was.
With only a sextant, Columbus could predict
An eclipse of the sun. Is it too late
To turn his sextant back upon a star

Luckier than the one he focused on?
Dali has left him little to navigate.
It's all hosannas, and Eden again, and a light
Silvering the sea, the innocent boys

Posturing as if it belonged to them.
He must have known they were far too young to be
What they purported to be. Are they *poseurs*?

Is this painting—the lances, the crosses, the ship—
Just another fabrication? Would he
Make a trip like this with men like *these*?

CONTENDING ANGELS

—a painting by Dali, 1950

Angels came down to meet the caravel—
High-born angels, angels with stones for eyes,
Their wings uneasy and fledgling, like pelicans
Diving into the wind. Their gowns reveal

Complexities of contour, colour and line.
Their dainty slippers, for example, make
Their legs too shapely for an angel to wear
On any beach, private or public. In fact,

Dali's angels seem to be parading
To catch the attention of sailors on the ship
Moored in a slip of white-water, between

Sloping cliffs, and a shoreline of shallow beach.
The hills beyond are terraced—or worn down
By cattle treading where other cattle trod.

THE DREAM

—an oil on canvas by Dali, 1937.

> *The visible world is no longer a reality*
> *and the unseen world is no*
> *longer a dream.*
> > —William Butler Yeats

> *The very dreams that blister sleep, boil*
> *up from the basic, magic ring of myth.*
> > —Joseph Campbell, *The Hero with*
> > *A Thousand Faces*, 1968.

With dreams like this, to be dead would be a dream
Devoutly to be wished. The crutches make
Self-motivated thought impossible.
Designed for walking, how long can they sustain

The weight of a whale immobilized in air?
In imitation of its master, a dog
Leans to the left, propped up on a single crutch.
Behind the dog, a man dressed like an Arab

Looks the other way. An abandoned boat
Drifts on the sands of time. A castle stands
Perforated with windows on an island

Unrelated, all by itself on a sea
Blue as the mist that's overtaking it,
The mist that turns all painting into dream.

THE BANKS OF THE OISE

—A rare landscape of the Ile de France
in which the décor consists only of
vegetation. The boats remind us of
what Signac did, which Rousseau
might have seen ten years before he
painted this oil on canvas, circa 1908.

> *Far from the birds, the flocks, the village life, ...*
> *Amidst the tender hazel copses ...*
> *What could I not quaff from the young Oise?*
> —Rimbaud

Had Columbus come into country like this—
Haystacks piled neatly, the harbour calm, the clouds
Twisting like corkscrews suggesting vineyards below,
The history of his voyage would have read

Not of something lost, but of something found.
He ran aground, instead, upon a land
Ignorant of Monet. The coast jungle
Stood there green and golden, (the sand, the trees)

But it was not Ile de France, not even Spain.
The two little boats in this painting seem content
To float forever on a pearly sea

Between haystacks and rows of poplar trees—
The kind of light that Monet would have loved
Had he been there in his little white boat.

IN ONE OF GOYA'S PAINTINGS

—based on a Goya painting of a dog
(1820) and one of Turner's paintings,
Dawn after the Wreck, 1840

In one of Goya's paintings, a little dog
Rises out of the mud banks of Madrid.
Its melancholy mouth, its mournful eyes
Express in paint the howling sentiment

Turner's dog is trying to express
All by itself on an empty strand, the sea
Lapping at the shores of its loneliness.
Nobody seems to know what Goya's dog

Symbolizes—as if it mattered to him,
Padding about nearly deaf, with his black paintings
Constantly on his mind. Did Turner's dog

Bay at the moon until the moon was lost
Behind a cloud? Or did it bay and bay
All day, all night, for what was missing at sea?

II

How strange it was: only a dog, and yet
Nothing is more appropriate than a dog
To keep the faith, to bay at the moon, until
The painter pays attention to its plight.

In one bold stroke, the painter eliminated
Empty gesture—the figures on the shore
That didn't believe in what they couldn't see.
Only the dog stayed awake for days, and searched

For distant lights, for the sight of a battered boat
Drifting out of the black and into the blue
Of early dawn. Only the dog remained

When everyone else had given up the search—
The sea turning green, then blue, then green, and then
Only the wind was howling, only the sea.

THE MOROCCAN TRIPTYCH OF 1912

—Three views of Tangier, including *The Open Window*,
Zorah on the Terrace, and *The Casbah Gate*, all from
the 1912 triptych commissioned by Morosov, now in
the Pushkin Museum.

Because of the open terraces, the walls,
The gleaming ramparts sloping down to the sea,
Windows are everywhere, and balconies—
Flowers in windows, pots on the windowsills.

Matisse must have carefully framed this view
By backing away from the open window. He saw
Trees and walls, a distant citadel,
A rabbits' warren of dark and narrow streets

Too intricate to penetrate from below.
From where he stood, a maze of buildings obscured
The hidden life of the city, hidden from those

Who didn't leave their slippers in neat rows
Outside of mosques, outside the blue café,
Where men sip tea and idly stare out of windows.

2. Zorah on the Terrace

Because of the icons, the French and Byzantine
Veiled icons, dignified ladies in gowns,
Matisse instinctively knew how to arrange
The Berber girl upon her pedestal,

Buttoned-up in a blue and white burnoose.
The plaster walls are more sky-blue than the sky
Her eyes are looking at, transfixed. A bowl
Brimming with goldfish stands within her reach,

Balanced on the pink of its pedestal.
So many goldfish! Beyond them is the sea.
They move around in their glass bubble, as if

Intent on being goldfish instead of paint.
She, too, will move around. She will dance to flutes.
Tomorrow night, she will walk through the casbah gate.

3. The Casbah Gate

Significant walls loom up behind the gate.
One-eyed birds in cages claw at the air.
Other birds are there for the taking. Her hair
Slides between her fingers. She pushes it back,

Tucks it tightly beneath her woolen shawl,
The nearly transparent, obligatory veil.
Night in the casbah. Smoke rises. The stars
Scatter light in the corners of crooked streets.

People pause when the singer in the tower
Intones the prayer that hovers in the air.
His silhouette is black against the sky.

Drums flare up as the king enters. His horse
Prances about on dainty feet, as if
Demonstrating the proper way to dance.

THE TERRACE, SAINT-TROPEZ

—an oil on canvas by Matisse, 1904

She shrugged and turned her head away, and said:
The Terrace, Saint-Tropez? What can I say?
She wouldn't speak of the painting by Matisse—
The windows blue, the water, the wooden fence

Between the clumps of bushes, and the sand
Beyond the balcony. It was too late
To go back to the terrace by the sea.
Even by taxi, the trip is impossible.

It's not here, she complained. *A big hotel—*
The taxi-driver interrupted: *It's true.*
My father used to tend to the gardens there,

The flowering vines, the roses. After the war—
It's always the war, another old lady said,
As if alluding to something tiresome.

BATHERS WITH A TURTLE

Based on *La Luxe* and *Bathers with a Turtle*, painted before and after Matisse went to Italy in 1907, this large oil on canvas, also known as *Three Women on the Edge of the Sea*, was begun by Matisse at the Couvent des Oiseaux, early in 1908.

Although there is no "official interpretation," this painting seems to suggest those musical contests between Apollo and Marsyas, Apollo and Pan. His adversaries played reed pipes, whereas Apollo—like Matisse—played a more "uplifting" stringed instrument.

In the myth of Apollo and Dryope, Apollo disguised himself as a turtle and let Dryope and her friends play with him. This is the myth Matisse refers to here, the myth upon which he has based his painting

> In <u>Bathers with a Turtle</u>, *image replaces text.*
> *Image and text are pulled apart, and the image*
> *that remains is as condensed as a poetic text.*
> —John Elderfield, 1992

The same year Matisse discovered Giotto
On a trip to Italy, he began
Exploring terrain that began with Paul Cézanne,
Continued with Picasso's *Desmoiselles*,

Culminating in *Bathers with a Turtle*—
"The birth of modern painting"; or did it mark
The end of an era begun in Perugia?
The bathers are bending over a turtle that

Bends time back into consciousness and beyond—
A parable of water and grass, a myth
Blatantly ambiguous. Perhaps

Matisse intends to exploit the *figure-ground*—
Apollo in a turtle-shell, his bride
Pearly-white on the edge of an incoming tide.

2. The turtle might have told them
   What it was like to be god-ridden and old.

Who took the flute, the turtle away from its myth?
Nobody did. Apollo abandoned the shell
He once inhabited. That left the girl—
The flautist sucking her fist—the other two

Toying with something that has a different play.
They don't know what to do. Their faces show
Consternation and fear, as one of them
Offers the turtle a wisp of a leaf, as if

That's all it takes to gratify a god.
If they had asked, the turtle might have said
Something timeless, something about the world

Reduced to color and light on an alien beach.
The turtle might have told them something about
What it was like to be god-ridden and old.

3. Gone are the dancers, the violins.

What it was like to be god-ridden and old
No longer seems to be relevant, to those
Standing apart from the grass they're standing on.
Perhaps they lost the key to the turtle's mouth.

The pressures of time and place: the shrinking earth,
Do the nurturing now—the sea behind
The standing central figure, the woman with
Toes turning inward, fingers that disappear.

They stand apart from what has gone before:
Pipes in the grass, the ring-dancing, the limbs
Clinging fast to a green, primordial tree.

Gone are the dancers, the violins. Each form
Stands by itself in time and space, as if
Free from the bondage of only being a part of.

4. Not even Pan stirs the grass.

Free from the bondage of being only a part of
Something larger, instrumental and bold,
All three women inhabit—in their way—
An undefined and indeterminate world.

There are no flutes. The turtle is a turtle,
Inclined to nibble on nothing—bits of fruit
Randomly picked and randomly arrayed
Upon a plate. Nothing is sacred here.

Nothing is worth the winning. The violin
Stays in its purple case. Not even Pan
Stirs the grass with a coarse and passionate cry.

There's hope, of course. It depends upon the leaf,
The tree it came from, the spirit of the gift—
Assuming the turtle is ready to speak of it.

5. He told us nothing because he wasn't asked.

Assuming the turtle is ready to speak of what
The sea cast up upon an alien beach,
There's hope, of course—depending upon the leaf,
The tree it came from, the spirit of the gift,

The instincts of the girls that reach for it.
Now they don't know what to do. They stand
Anguished and astonished at the turtle
Red and segmented, god-ridden and old,

Reduced to color and light upon the sand.
It's strange to think our lives depend upon
What happens to a stranded turtle, a shell

Red and segmented, god-ridden and old—
Who told us nothing, because he wasn't asked
Why Apollo was posing as a turtle.

74

NUDE WITH A TAMBOURINE

—American art critic Frankfurter
compared this painting to Matisse's
The Statue, 1916: Its echo in the
marvelous heavy impasto developed
in 1926, brilliant in great surfaces
like the lode of a rare jewel....

Tearing himself essentially free of art—
Those lines of force that so intensely held
Painter and man together, he began
Searching her flesh for signs of another world,

The world her body suggested. After all,
She didn't ask to arrange herself that way—
Her left arm raised, her breast lifted, her foot
Tucked in at the ankle under her knee.

The tambourine behind her on the couch
Anticipates the flaming at her feet.
Her skin, in turn, excited the steady gleam

Elastic in the tambourine: it leaps
Off the couch in a sudden motion, as she
Reaches over to bang it, elbow and fist.

II

The rich red thick and heavy impasto paint
Laid on like paste, teeming with images,
Must have reminded the painter of that glow
Green in Ravenna, blue in Venetia

At the Piazza San Marco: the gilded cross,
The crowns of the fourteen virgins in a row,
The gold mosaics, the rubies, the emeralds—
Not to speak of the icons lost in the wars,

The stone-cutters, the villagers gone to ground
Between the church and the tower. Matisse was told
Stories about the pillaging, the ships

Fleeing by sea, their rigging on fire, and how
They drove the mounted invader into the swamps,
Their salt-infested bones still floating there.

III

Now the last of the virgins, her tambourine
Quivering as it used to quiver, the nude
Poses alone and unselfconsciously.
Her pose suggests she knows what she's about—

A half-blind window behind her, framing a sky
Blurred by blue, the only blue still extant
Untouched by time, the ravages of youth;
And then, of course, the wallpaper, the couch—

The doting armchair, her other lover, its arms
Holding her firm but secure, encircling her—
Guarding each bone, each stone in her diadem.

How much of the past can be put into one nude
No matter how comely, how riveting the mood
The painter creates with nothing but color and light?

Contemplating the Seashore. Photo by L.A. Larrabee

THE BLONDE BATHER OF PROVENCE AND POMPEII

—from the painting by Auguste Renoir

Her body was his, but her eyes belonged to the sea.
He must have seen what she was seeing, when
He painted her blonde against the blue, her hair
Glistening gold and windblown. Seated that way

She looked like the girl in the fresco in Pompeii
The painter had seen reclining on a wall:
Her burnished hair a newly minted coin
Dropped by the sun, and caught in the mouth of a wave

That sealed her smile and lacquered her flesh with ashes.
Renoir must have recognized that look
When he saw her smiling: the same look

She was wearing later, her back to the sea—
The same sea, but twenty centuries later,
When loved and painted (perhaps) by the same painter.

THE HARBOUR AT BORDEAUX

—an oil on canvas by Edouard Manet, 1871

Painted from a café window, this scene
Must have enchanted Manet: a maze of masts
Competing with distant cathedral spires.
It must be dawn. The men are rolling casks

Down to the dock for loading. In the boats,
Sails are being hoisted, the rigging set.
Other boats are waiting to take their turn
Along the dock, where stacks of cargo stand

Untouched as yet. What are they waiting for—
The sun to increase the pace of activity?
Perhaps the men are still at breakfast, where

The air is thick with smoke from briar pipes.
The coffee urns are steaming. One by one,
They gulp the last *calvados* on the run.

BOULOGNE HARBOUR BY MOONLIGHT

—an oil on canvas by Manet, 1869

Huddled together, the womenfolk wait
For the return of their men. The tide is in.
Boats are rocking gently at anchor, their masts
Silhouetted and peaceful, as they float

Upon the harbour's mirrored surface. The moon
Benignly breaks through clouds, as if to say:
Why worry? The women know better, they
Know how late the boats are. In their bones,

They know things that the moon has always ignored.
The brilliant stars mean nothing. Out to sea,
The swells could be surging, their husbands tossed about

Even as they are huddled together, waiting.
The torch in the tower is lit. What more can they do?
In dark houses, slender widows are snoring.

ON THE BEACH

—In this seascape, an oil on canvas
Manet painted at Berck in Normandy
during the summer of 1873, he used
his wife and his brother as models
for the figures on the beach.

In this important study of water and light,
His wife and his brother were the models for
The two figures reclining on the shore.
In front of them, the sea is rolling in—

A few quick strokes of white on blue and green,
As if the painter had reached over, and put
The water in, the boats above their heads,
The vast expanse of sand along the shore.

Because they, too, were pigment, they didn't flinch
When his brush grazed them, left them saturated—
Especially his wife, hunched over in her hood,

A dumpy mound of brown reading a book.
It was as if she had nothing to do but pose
Upon a barren beach in evening clothes.

2. From side to side, a dark flotilla floats

They're more pigment than people, as they pose
Upon a barren beach in evening clothes.
Yet they seem rooted, deeply rooted, as if
To move a foot would be an enormous task.

Propped up on an elbow, the brother seems
Unaware of the boats in front of him.
From side to side, a dark flotilla floats—
Navigates in the deep water across

The upper part of this abstract painting, as if
Another kind of sea were surging there.
Nor does Suzanna seem likely to look up,

So rooted is she in what she is reading, her foot
Wedged into sand like a sand-turtle, an egg
More *Fabergé* than what a real egg is.

3. Are they but figments, rooted in color?

He painted her encased in a veil, her eyes
Slits in a peep-hole, a woman reading a book,
A ribbon knotting her bonnet in the back.
The other figure, draped in a cape that sports

Black and white stripes on its collar and its cuff,
Is leaning back with his eyes closed, facing the sea.
Although composed, they hardly seem to be
Acclimated to beach-life in July.

Yet they seem rooted, deeply rooted in sand,
As if to move would be an enormous task.
Where would they go? What would they do? The sea

Doesn't seem ready to wash their sins away.
Are they but figments rooted in color, their flesh
Laid on lightly, perfected by trial and error?

82

4. It mingles with light, was meant to mingle

It's all surface. How can a surface portray
Anything more than what it's meant to be?
How can this pigment, laid on a gesso base,
Transform an inert plant-fiber, a flat

Unassuming canvas? After all,
It's not flesh—it's only canvas here,
A deaf and dumb and blind repository
Only the young and mindless can safely ignore,

Instinctively reject. The color's right.
It mingles with light, was *meant* to mingle and make
A sky stay put where the painter put it, a sea

Suspend itself in painterly delight.
From side to side, a dark-skinned fleet of boats
Navigates night in an empty, meaningless search.

5. The kind of sun-shot waves that ducks adore

Although Manet despised the open air,
A part of this was painted where they were—
Grains of sand embedded in the paint.
How long did he have to stand there? Did the wind

Tug at his easel? Did he tie it down
As Monet had to do at Entretat?
His wife and his brother seem resigned
To posing in the same position forever.

Just offshore, some fishing boats went by—
Their sails cut close the sky, the picture frame,
Tacking their way across a patch of grey.

But closer in, the waves are lazy and green—
The kind of sun-shot waves that ducks adore,
Diving for fish that flash along the shore.

LOBSTER AND CAT ON THE BEACH

—an oil on canvas by Picasso, dated
Mougins, 14 January 1965.

Sea battles—: the lions of Skeleton Beach
That feast on seals, and prowl the sand-dunes, as
The sky lets fire down. These battles reach
Strange proportions—not just the lion, but

The water-holes behind them in the brush
Blood-encrusted, the mud stirred up by hooves,
A cross-hatching of tracks begun before
These young lions arrived. Their fathers were

Fossilized for a million years, before
The weather changed, the food-chain disappeared.
Now it's a lobster and cat. Why not a cock

To round the picture out? The sea's the same—
The same old sand, the same old sun, the blood
Locked in battle on such a pleasant day.

BEACH SCENE

—detail from a painting by Degas,
1876, now in the National Gallery,
London. This painting—an oil and
essence on paper mounted on canvas—
separates objects, as in Japanese prints.

> *When somebody asked Degas how he*
> *painted this picture, he answered: 'I*
> *spread my flannel vest on the floor*
> *of the studio, and had the model sit*
> *on it. You see, the air you breathe*
> *in a picture is not necessarily the*
> *same as the air out of doors'.*
> —quoted in Bade's *Degas*, 1991

Shadowless, these figures walk on sand, or sit
As if they were timeless—or on a different beach
Than this unmoving, relentless play upon
A bland and empty, stark sensation of sun.

High on the left are white-robed figures that slink
Out of the painting, as if they were visitors
Belonging to another era—: a Greek
Temple-frieze, a Roman family outing.

Behind these figures wrapped in towels are three
Cartoon figures: a man with a cane, a dog,
A woman with a closed umbrella. But two—

A girl and her maid—dominate front and center.
Head and hands are linked together, as one
Draws a small comb through the hair of the other.

APPROACHING STORM

—an oil on panel, 1864, by
Eugene Boudin (1824–1898),
a teacher of Claude Monet. His
beach scenes demonstrate the
play of light in nature.

Who is this woman in white who stands apart—
The shocking white of her white, billowing gown,
Her jacket trimmed in black, her black felt hat,
Her white umbrella, her shaggy little dog

That leads the way across the sandy beach?
The child beside her (dressed alike) is white—
But not as white as the woman and the dog.
Is she attracting, or blunting the great storm

Gathering dark and blue over her shoulder?
The sky is intensely dark and blue. The clouds
Blot up the blue as if they were blotting paper.

But nothing, nothing is whiter than her gown—
The woman in white, the woman who stands apart.
She alone ignores the oncoming storm.

II

Sixteen figures surround the woman in white—
Women in stripes in beach chairs, women with shawls,
Women huddled together in bonnets and gowns.
All appear apprehensive. An old sailor

Alarms the women by pointing at the storm.
The wind is tugging at feathers, ribbons and bows.
A flag is flapping. The women gesticulate
The woman in white ignores the idle chatter.

She alone is standing in the sun.
The storm's behind her. She doesn't turn around,
But treats the storm as if it doesn't exist.

She carries her umbrella like a walking stick.
She leans on it imperiously, a queen
Who may or may not deign to open it.

GREEN SEA

—an oil on canvas, 1976,
By Philip Guston (1913–1980)

> "*Green Sea* is one of a series of
> paintings (Philip) Guston did in
> 1976 featuring a tangle of disem-
> bodied legs, bent at the knees and
> wearing flat, ungainly shoes, grouped
> on the horizon of a deep green sea
> against a salmon-colored backdrop ...
> Its meaning eludes us."
> > —descriptive note, *Master Paintings*
> > *in the Art Institute of Chicago*

The meaning of *horseshoe* eludes the rider, who sits
Far off the ground, his feet never touching
The rock the hoof strikes, steel on stone, the spark
Igniting momentarily the twig

Dry in the dust, waiting for something like this.
Of course the meaning of this painting eludes us.
Our shoes have never looked like this, our knees
Never bent at angles as blunt as these—

Nor are they so knobby. Boot-heels or horseshoes,
How many closets collect such crude antiques?
Who would discard them to float on a green sea?

Guston would and did. Disembodied legs?
The bodies must have been truly something to see—
The kind of thing you would bury standing up.

TAHITIAN SKETCHES

These four sketches are based on four oil
paintings by Paul Gauguin in the order that
they appear: 1. *Leaping into the Sea*, 1892;
2. *Man with an Axe*, 1891; 3. *Tahitian Landscape*, 1893;
and, 4. *Words the Devil Said* (*Paradise Lost*), 1892

> *I cannot grasp your art.*
> *I cannot like it.*
> *I cannot get a grip on your art,*
> *Which is so exclusively Tahitian.*
> > —letter from playwright
> > August Strindberg to
> > Paul Gauguin, 1895

1. Leaping into the Sea

Three are leaning into a green abyss:
One on shore, one in the water, and one
Ready to leap, leaping into the sea.
The girl on shore unveils her nakedness,

The mystery of her flesh before she dives.
Dives into what? These apparitions make
Demands upon the metaphysical—
Colors that Strindberg never knew, before

He looked at this, and doubted what he had seen.
The cresting waves, the flowers on the shore
Echo each other—the flower-shapes that fall

Upon the bathers lying under a tree.
Delicious fruit is ripening in the sun.
Their bodies glisten like polished ebony.

2. Man with an Axe

Here it began: the man with the axe, a boat
Sliding by with a single sail, the wind
Barely brushing the surface of the sea.
He saw it all when he arrived: the man

Chopping wood, the woman behind him, the tide.
He painted a landscape later, a year later,
Using the stance of the axe man, not the stroke—
And peacocks, flaunting their tail-feathers, and girls

Flouncing away in missionary dresses.
Behind the man, a woman is storing nuts
In the prow of a burly dugout canoe.

Gauguin could see her moving from his hut—
The door open, the smell of fish and salt
Thick in the mist that floated off the shore.

3. Tahitian Landscape

It was enough to go walking out of sight,
The fish on a pole that swings at every step,
The fruit in the bag that dangles. Where was he
Before he caught the sunfish on the beach,

The fruit along the way? The path he takes
Leads nowhere—a cleft between the rock
That opens into another open space.
The sweat-band in his hat is leather. His shoes

Stick to his feet and stain the bottoms blue.
Better to go barefoot, the natives say.
And so he does—as if the natives knew

What to do about parasites in the feet,
The friendly beasts that walk along with you.
He thought it was the price you had to pay.

4. *Paradise Lost*

It's not too hard to imagine losing this.
They never had it, consciously. It just
Flared up, flowered and fell. It disappeared—
Evaporated, some say, at the height—

A pure apotheosis, a paradise
Unsurpassed by any conscious thought.
Dante couldn't imagine what he missed:
The breadfruit tree, the mango, the sandy beach

Never lapped by the waters of Italy.
And England's harsh implacability—
The fog by night, the cloud-cover by day

Didn't inspire Milton to the heights
That really existed, that flared up, flowered and fell
In a far country that didn't know it was lost.

THE LAST OF ENGLAND

—an oval oil on canvas by
Ford Madox Brown, 1852–5,
now in the Birmingham Museum.
This painting, based on the theme
of middle-class emigration, was
inspired by Thomas Woolmans'
departure for Australia in
July 1852

They left it all behind to emigrate
To land more sympathetic to their aims—
A plot of land, the right to move about
As free men could where land was plentiful

And names were only names. The boats were full
Of men and women like these—and children, too—
Huddled together, hunched down against the wind
That tested them whatever way it could.

The ropes and eye-hooks in this painting show
Fish in a net, the noose of helplessness
That tightened about them whatever way they moved

Yet they knew—they banked on it, wave by wave—
The end of it was sufficient to endure
The perilous voyage, the agonized departure.

The Brooklyn Bridge, 2000. Photo by L.A. Larrabee

THE BROOKLYN BRIDGE

—based on an oil on canvas by Joseph Stella, 1918–19, now at Yale University.
Stella's painting, *The Bridge*, inspired Hart Crane's long poem, "The Bridge"

> *Through the bound cable strands, the arching path*
> *Upward, veering with light, the flight of strings,—*
> *Taut miles of shuttling moonlight syncopate*
> *The whispered rush, telepathy of wires.*
> > —Hart Crane

> *Many nights I stood on the bridge—and in the middle alone—lost—a*
> *defenseless prey to the surrounding swarming darkness—crushed by the*
> *mountainous black impenetrability of the skyscrapers....*
> *Now and then strange moanings of appeal from tugboats, guessed more than*
> *seen, through the infernal recesses below—I felt deeply moved, as if on the*
> *threshold of a new religion or in the presence of a new DIVINITY.*
> > —Joseph Stella,
> > "Brooklyn Bridge: A Page of My Life"

This is not a romantic bridge of sighs,
A golden gate looping over the blue Pacific.
Stella's bridge is a muscular bridge, its thick
Understructure and piers, its watchful eyes

Scan the river like an Irish cop. Hart Crane
Numbered its strands, took solace in the water
Veering with light and the flight of quivering strings
Where Sibylline voices flicker. Did he stop

To wonder what became of the marshy shores—
The Iroquois camps, the teepees, the fishing huts
Inundated by skyscrapers and piers?

Did he stand on the bridge as Stella did,
Deeply moved, as if on the threshold of
A new religion, a new DIVINITY?

II

Stella reported standing on the bridge
Trembling all over with emotion. He had
Days of anxiety, torture, and delight
As he stood there responding to the sight:

Many nights I stood on the bridge alone,
Aware of the *strange moanings of appeal—*
From tugboats, guessed more than seen. Imagine
Stella standing there, "trembling all over,"

Gripped by a cacophony "guessed more than seen
Through the infernal recesses below."
Who are these men who sense what others don't,

Who tremble "all over" at the sound
Of "strange moanings" that others do not hear?
Are they still around? Are they still standing here?

III

Down at water-level, beneath a pier,
A man is standing on a wooden deck
Watching the sky for signs. Around him swirl
Countless seagulls, waiting for the dawn,

The daily ritual. He feeds them bread.
They know this man. They take it out of his hand.
Loaf after loaf, he flings it into the air.
Then he sits there, lights his pipe, and enjoys

Choirs of river-rats, lined up on the piers.
He seems to like nature, the sights and sounds
Other men ignore. Who is this man—

Ostensibly a bridge-tender, sweeping the decks
Beneath an airy bridge for twenty years?
Is he more? Is he a man like Stella?

IV

Down from the mountains of Italy, Stella and he
May have something in common. He cultivates
The flocks of seagulls swirling down, the flash
Of sunlight in their wings. He knows by heart

The eerie songs of the river-rat, the sound—
Of tugboats in fog: "moanings guessed more than seen."
Does it matter he doesn't have the words
To write an epic about the Brooklyn Bridge

"Veering with light, where Sibylline voices flicker"?
Who knows what he sees, or what he thinks about?
Ultimately, it doesn't matter, but here

Hart Crane stood, and Joseph Stella, who made
Something out of nothing but color and light—
And in so doing, they left something behind.

V

He painted what he felt and framed it, and here
Stella's bridge transfigures color and light—
Its Gothic towers gleaming as they did
When he came on the scene. How much of it

Stands by itself? How much is projection:
"Days of anxiety, torture, and delight?"
Both are prismatic—the bridge and Stella—they burn
Red at the center, red at the base of what

Drives the bridge upward, shores it up into light
As if it were glad to be uplifted in air.
Cool at the top, the eyes of its towers are blue—

Calm and secure that in this perilous world
The bridge will stand—the strands and cables will hold
As if suspended by more than Gothic towers.

THE OLD LIGHTHOUSE

—based on *The Lighthouse*, an etching
by Edward Hopper, 1923

The yellow shutters, the catwalk and the light
Beguile the eye unaccustomed to the quirks
Of coastal life, the eccentricities
That send a boat at midnight into the mist.

The lightning rods on the tower ground the strikes
Seeking combat, but sliding down the glass
To find another target less alert.
All night, all day, the yellow light revolves.

It sings a yellow song. It casts an eye
Where nothing but a piercing yellow light
Can penetrate. It stands up to the dark,

Not unlike the luminous knight that charged
Things that stirred beyond the range of his lance—
Distant things, that dance in their own orbits.

II

Eternally remote, this yellow light
Glitters through sheets of cut-glass as it glares
Into the murky night. It swivels on
Its own internal mechanism, a bright

Wheel of fortune that glitters as it spins—
An isle of light, a bright oasis, that
Radiates hope when hope is running low.
Whose land is this? What light is looming up?

It swivels and blurs and flashes as if on cue,
Cutting through layers of fog and yellow mist—
A yellow eye, that winks and winks and winks

Until a horn is heard. Are there still ships
Spinning in circles, lost in the rushing tide,
Searching for the slightest sign of a light?

GROUNDSWELL OFF NANTUCKET

—based on Hopper's oil on canvas, *Ground Swell,* 1939

Rather than putting the boat about, they tried
Riding it out against the oncoming wave,
Their prow too high in the water for the next
Punishing blow that caught them in a trough.

Ride it out, the captain shouted, and leaned
Into the wind, the lusty wind from the east.
Take it about, he shouted, and they heeled
Away from the black bell-buoy, and its bell

Telling them what they knew too well already.
The sea is marble. The boat is marble. The men
Stare at the sea with stone expressions. They know

What can happen in swells, when the sea demands
Heroic measures, the ultimate command
No man can ignore—not even the captain.

ROCKY COVE

—a watercolor on paper by Edward Hopper, 1929

This looks like the cove in which the world began.
Be kind to it. Its life-span might be yours.
Let's look at it closer, the way the picture-painter
Might have looked when he painted the three rocks

Large and dark in the foreground. Why do they
Cluster together like stony-boats, their bulk
Reminiscent of elephant seals, of whales?
A trinity of equal parts, they lie

Bundled together like old theology—
Like Dead Sea scrolls, like bottles dropped by a star.
Beyond the rocks is Landfall, a sandy beach.

Beyond the beach is a meadow, and a sky
Hovering over the red roof of a house
Too far away to know if it's empty or not.

BOATS AT LES TROIS-
SAINTES-MARIES-DE-LA-MER

—an oil on canvas by Van Gogh, 1888.
On this beach the Gypsies hold their annual
pilgrimage in May, commemorating the
story of the three Marys (trios Saintes-Maries),
and their Gypsy handmaid, Sara, who helped
them escape from Jerusalem.

—What strikes me here, and what
makes painting so attractive is the
clearness of the air …

I have only been here a few months,
but tell me this—could I, in Paris, have
done the drawing of the boats in an hour?
Even without the respective frame, I do it
now without measuring, just by letting
my pen go …
            —Letter to Wilhelmina, 1888

In this boat, the one with fish-eyes, the three
Marys went out to argue with the sea—
One at the bow, another at the oars,
The third at the rudder, steering with her feet,

Ducking the main-sail each time it came about.
That's how they spoke of it among themselves—
First at the Horse Fair, and later, in the crypt,
While pinning up votives on the Tree of Tatters—

A sock from a crushed foot, an eye-patch from a man
Touched by the water that gave him eyes again;
The grips of an old crutch, a silken handkerchief

Streaked with the tokens of a widow's grief.
And then, at dawn, the candles guttering—
The Gypsies carry their Sara into the sea.

THE BANQUET OF THE CIVIC GUARD,
JUNE 18ᵗʰ, 1648, TO CELEBRATE
THE PEACE OF MUNSTER, 1648

—When Vermeer was seven, Spain lost
the Netherlands. In the sea-battle of the
Downs, 1639, Dutch Admiral Tromp
annihilated the Spanish fleet—Tromp's
13 ships against 20,000 men and 77 ships.
Bartholomeus van der Helst's painting
shows the Amsterdam Civic Guard, nine
years later, celebrating the Treaty of Münster
with a typically boisterous banquet.

Ignoring war, they celebrated the peace
By having their portraits painted—gilded frames
Vying with tapestries on the whitewashed walls.
This was the age of the proud, the pious, the pure—

Men who look down at us from the portraits they paid for,
Their sons looking up at them, as they once looked up
To their fathers before them, who had grown
Impressively stout and prosperous. Their wits

Made them as rich in peacetime as in war.
They didn't need it anymore, to make
Open sea-lanes, their cities safe from attack,

Their ships in harbours, heavy with marble and fish,
With Persian rugs and silk and satin and teak—
Delftware, spices, and Chinese porcelain.

MUNCH'S MELANCHOLY OF 1896

—a woodcut now in Oslo that derives from
the 1892–3 paintings of *Melancholy*, same
title, different dates. Munch made many
variations on this theme in oil and woodcut.

> *Down here on the beach I seem*
> *to find an image of my-*
> *self—of my life—*
> *Is it because*
> *it was by the beach*
> *we walked together that day?*
> > —Edvard Munch

Again he is sitting there, solitary and stern.
The figure by the water's edge, looks out
Upon a rippled reflection of itself.
Cloudy of brow and impulsive, it reflects

More than sky, the curling lip of the wave
Impatient to be running up the shore.
It cries out. It even roars, when the wind
Finds the rigging it used to give concerts in.

The figure on the shore is thinking thoughts
Rooted in wave-curl, the seaweed boiling up
Beneath a shuddering hull. Does it recall

The bent oar, the hollow knock of oarlock,
The fishy smell of a foreign port, the noose
Phosphorescent around the ocean's throat?

THE VOICE

In *Epipsychidion,* Przybyszewski speaks of an
enticing, mysterious voice on the beach at night:

*Then I knew! It was the voice with bleeding
eyes that I was searching for. It was the sea ... the
voice of the sea.*

Tied up by fate and something else unseen,
She stands erect, her hands behind her back—
A panther pacing behind the verticals
Of a panther cage. And yet she stands

As if she could snap her handcuffs, leap into space—
Pretending, now, to be helpless on a beach
Where ships go by. Helen of Troy? The voice
Ulysses fought his ropes for, stuffed his ears?

Her eyes are dark. Contempt has made them burn
Brighter than what they really are, and yet
It's not her eyes that matter, it's the voice

Throbbing as the sea throbs in its sleep—
The voice that sings of forgotten things, the voice
Ulysses fought his ropes for, stuffed his ears.

THE DOVE FROM THE ARK

—*la columbe de l'arche,* an etching
and drypoint by Marc Chagall, 1956

Then they began to keep the dove in a jar
Built like a tabernacle, radiant—
A milky, transparent, two-way silhouette
Suggesting a window, a miracle, a door

Off its hinges, translucent, invisible—
A non-existent barrier that stood
In the Divine Center, like a *bimah*
Erected by Noah where the Pilot House

Used to be, before a dove was discovered
Walking around the poop deck, picking up corn—
As if it were really a dove, and not a sign

Straight from a distant alcove to an ark
Desolate without a dove to believe in,
A dove to launch like a spaceship into the stars.

IN THE NEIGHBORHOOD OF VENCE

—an oil on canvas by Marc Chagall, 1957

These sights and sounds in the belly of a whale
Huge enough to float the universe,
Settle down to infinite bouquets—
Snow White candles, and waves as red as love

That stain the beaches of a marble sky
Theologically different than the world
They occupy. Here ladders and stairways are
Invisible and everywhere. They rise

Out of the ribcage of a flying fish
Where Christ is resurrecting in the flesh—
Up a tower, down a pear tree, where

Lovers are embracing in the air.
This ark is expanding to such enormous size,
It's making the sky seem irreversibly blue.

Drawing by D. George

THINKING ABOUT WILD GEESE GOING OVER

—from a hand scroll in ink, color and gold
on paper, *Wang Hsi-chih Watching Geese*
by Ch'ien Hsüan, c. 1235—after 1301.

> *Wild geese have no intent to cast reflection;*
> *Water has no mind to receive their image.*
>   —from a fortune-cookie

I do not think wild geese intend to cast
Reflections on still water, nor does the water
Intend to bend these images still further,
Unless the mind of water reflects its past—

If water has a mind of its own. When last
Released, it seemed to brood. Behind its breath
A mind began to move with a steady stealth
Of wind rising, and rain, and then a blast

That made a sea of sky and land, until
The wild geese going over had no place
To rest. Perhaps the geese, like mind itself,

Are superimposed upon a concept of space
Where nothing in time is missing or amiss—
And water exists to darkly reflect the geese.

SKY AND WATER I

In this woodcut of 1938, Escher's description of his intention greatly enhances what he achieved:

> *In the horizontal central strip there*
> *are birds and fish equivalent to each*
> *other. We associate flying with sky,*
> *and so for each of the black birds the*
> *sky in which it is flying is formed by*
> *the four white fish which encircle it.*
> *Similarly, swimming makes us think*
> *of water, and therefore the four black*
> *birds that surround a fish become the*
> *water in which it swims.*

They swim and fly in each other's elements,
As they must have done a long time before
Escher thought of it. These primitive fish
Fall so easily out of sky, that they

Seem to be born to it. The whites of their eyes
Carry the sky about with them. Their fins
Still resemble the wings they wore, before

They tumbled out of air, and left the sun
Sailing far behind. Isn't it strange
To see the swans in rising out of a sea

Darker even than they are, black on white—
A sea that stains what it touches, as they fly
Whiter and whiter against a liquid sky?

THE RIPPLED SURFACE

Escher's remarks about this linocut printed from two blocks (1950) are characteristic about his concerns as a graphic artist:

> *The rings shown in perspective afford the only means whereby the receding surface of the water is indicated.*

Two raindrops, falling into a pond,
Become the pond that they are falling on—
Become the moon, the tree, the tangled limbs
Intertwined with broken rings, and the rain

That left two drops behind. How soon will they
Assimilate with what they have become—
Give up their rings, their ripples that the wind
Will smooth with its white hand? Already, they

Are slowing down their microscopic sense
Of oceanic pride. Their ripples are
Running out of steam, the inner surge,

The energetic sense of what they were
Before they fell upon a tranquil pond
That once was still, will soon be still again.

THOUGHTS IN THE SISTINE CHAPEL

—from the fresco by Michelangelo

There, on the ceiling, God's finger reaching out
Nearly touches Adam's finger, yet
Why the distance? Why did he hesitate?
Why, in that instant, did He prefer to be

Insulated by distance, by the dance
Shifting its weight with one foot in the flesh,
The other in the backwash of the sea?
In that instant, a narwhale came to rest.

A dinosaur unfurled its length of bone.
In that instant, another beast was born
To take its place upon a human breast.

Nothing is impossible. The least is most.
And most of all are the swallows who perch on stone—
Build their nests, and nestle bone to bone.

SHE KEEPS HER SECRET

—a pencil, frottage on gouache
production by Max Ernst, 1925

Naturally, she keeps her secret within
The fossil she has become, the withered shell
Open to wind and other alien ears.
How else can a fossil survive in fossildom?

The balancing is no act. It is a fact
She stands that way, perfectly upright, to hear
Whatever a shell needs to hear to stay alive.
She also needs to decipher what is writ

Upon her bone, her porcelain overcoat—
The secret signs, the hieroglyphic notes
Fossils carry about from time to time.

She has become her own time-keeper, her own
Spirit-tender upon a treacherous slope.
Against all odds, she has become heroic.

THE ESCAPER

—a frottage by Max Ernst, from his
"Histoire Naturelle"

Floating above the tiles of the ocean floor—
Patio-tiles, long stepped on, and erased
By those who came before and after (perhaps)—
A sea-monster, a truly enormous fish

Is fixing the painter with an insolent stare.
What did the painter think when it swam by,
Its scales and plates like Dürer's rhinoceros?
Finless, except for prehensile hands and feet—

A breathing flap, a rudimentary beak,
How did the painter deal with its glassy eye?
More like a wheel (the rose window at Chartres?)

Its eye is neither fish nor fowl. It seems
The kind of eye encountered in a dream—
Unremitting in its intensity.

THE TURBULENT SEA AT ETRETAT

—based on *Rough Sea at Etretat*
by Claude Monet (1840–1926) and
The Cliff at Etretat after the Storm by
Gustave Courbet (1819–1877); also these
paintings by Monet: *The Cliff at Etretat*
(1883) and *The Lily-pond* (1910).

> *Monet is no more than an eye—*
> *but, my god, what an eye!*
> —Cézanne's famous
> comment about Monet

The sea was rough that day at Etretat—
The waves six deep, and higher than the eye
Could see over, if standing on the shore.
The wind that was hurling waves upon the rocks,

Billowed the skirts of village women, who were
Standing among the villagers. The men
Seem to be angry, their boots stamping the sand,
As if contending with the relentless wind,

The sea that was raging for no reason at all.
One was still looking for the little boat
Lost at sea, his hand up, shielding his eyes—

As if he were saluting. Is that why Monet
Painted the windswept beach at Etretat—
The waves cresting, the white spray on the rock?

II

Courbet's beach at Etretat was calm.
The stinging spray Monet had encountered there—
The booming surf, the crashing waves, were gone.
The rocky face of the cliff was dark, where they

Had left their mark upon the polished rock.
What motivated Monet to paint a sea
Volatile and raging? Did he believe
The soul of the sea was cresting? Did each wave

Become a revelation, an oracle?
In tide is change. The raging heart of time
Thumps and thunders before it settles down,

Becomes the beach that Courbet painted—the calm
Sun-baked rock and fishing boats, high on the sand,
The waves lapping, the water tender and green.

III

There are no people here, only the boats—
Tackle and gear piled neatly, nets and oars
Roped to the anchor rope. The emptiness
Must have startled Courbet—or did he think

Nothing is empty, there is no empty thing?
The way he painted the sky, the rocks, the sea—
Each cloud and weed, each blade of grass, each grain
Committed the painter to painting what he saw

In raw reality. As Ingres said,
"Courbet is an eye." Courbet studied the scene,
And what he saw became a monument.

Not so Monet, who painted what became
Impressionistic, ever-changing light—
As if the sea reflected upon itself.

IV

The sea he painted became his private pond.
Lily-pads floated where Courbet saw only weed.
He painted the lily-pads from a little boat
That floated around and around. Monet believed

Color and light were their own authorities.
When he caught light moving, he painted it
Before it could get away. Monet believed
He had to act, to catch it moving, before

It changed back into what it was before
He painted it. Unlike Monet, Courbet
Believed that light was a definite entity.

The shape of it, Courbet thought, was in the eye—
Not in the object itself, for that would be
A never-ending, changing reality.

V

A never-ending beach? A storm at sea?
The people Monet had painted must have dispersed.
Courbet's painting had no people. There were
Fishing boats, and whitewashed rocks, and grass

Monet had no room for on his palette.
Perhaps at Giverny—in his little boat—
Monet would think about the universe.
Perhaps the sea at Etretat would be

A particle of light that he had seen
Lurking behind a lily-pad in the rain.
Did not his little garden and his pond

Encapsulate the origins of light?
For twenty years he painted lilies there
The green expanses, the whitely scattered stars.

MONET'S LAST REQUEST

—based on a Manet seascape
and a poignant letter to Renoir

Born of the sea, a child of harbour and shore,
He tested the air with a wet finger—
And sniffed it for the scent as a hound-dog does,
The lifelong habit of the Norman sailor.

When I die, he said of the sea he loved,
I want to be buried in a bobbing buoy—
Not in the village churchyard in a box.
But there he is, the iron tongue of God

Muffled by sod, a gravestone over his head.
How often does the sea come up the Seine
To where his boat is moored in its private pond?

Perhaps he senses the algae in the shade,
The turtles and frogs that nestle in the reeds,
The lily-pads, the lilies in the rain.

In the Mouth of the Whale. Photo by L.A. Larrabee

INDEX TO TITLES OF POEMS

120

INDEX TO FIRST LINES OF POEMS

124

978-0-595-44227-0
0-595-44227-7